PROFILES

Mother Teresa

Mary Craig

Illustrated by
Janet Fahy

Hamish Hamilton
London

For my cousin, Anne Forbes, with love

First published 1983 by
Hamish Hamilton Children's Books
Garden House, 57-59 Long Acre, London WC2E 9JZ
© text 1983 by Mary Craig
© illustrations 1983 by Janet Fahy
Reprinted 1983, 1984
All rights reserved
Reprinted 1985

British Library Cataloguing in Publication Data
Craig, Mary
Mother Teresa.
1. Teresa, *Mother*   2. Nuns–Calcutta (India)–
Biography
I. Title
266′.2′0924   BX4705.T4455
ISBN 0-241-10933-7

Typeset by Pioneer
Printed in Great Britain at the
University Press, Cambridge

Contents

1 An Albanian Childhood

On 27 August 1910 a daughter was born to an Albanian couple living in Skopje, Macedonia, which was later to become part of Yugoslavia. The child was christened Gonxha (Agnes) Bejaxhiu, a name less easy for Western tongues to pronounce than the one by which she came to be known all over the world — Mother Teresa of Calcutta.

The Albanians living in Skopje were a very close-knit group who kept their own language and traditions alive in a foreign land. Some were Moslems, some Orthodox Christians. But the Bejaxhiu family had been Roman Catholics for generations.

Gonxha had a sister Aga, who was five years older than she was, and a brother Lazar, who was two years older. Two sisters born after Gonxha died as babies. Their father, Nikola, co-owned a building firm in Skopje and the family was fairly well-off. Nikola was an Albanian patriot who dreamed of freedom for his country and he filled his house with nationalists like himself. One night he came home from a political meeting complaining that he felt ill. He collapsed, was rushed off to the hospital, and died a few hours later. The other Albanians all believed that he had been poisoned by his political enemies.

Suddenly the family had lost its breadwinner. But Nikola's widow, Dronda, was not daunted. She started a small embroidery business to support the family and keep it together. Though the children's father had died, Dronda saw to it that they were happy and cared for.

Gonxha and her sister were very fond of each other and they shared a passion for music. They both belonged to the church choir and also to the Skopje Albanian youth choir in which Gonxha frequently sang solo. On outings with the family or with friends she would accompany herself on the accordion or the mandolin.

Mrs Bejaxhiu was as deeply religious as her husband had been political. Where once the house had been full of noisy Albanian patriots, it was now more like a religious centre. Both girls shared their mother's enthusiasm for the work of the Church and they loved to meet the missionaries who talked of the far-off lands where they worked. Some of these had gone from Yugoslavia to India, and it was their stories which particularly enthralled Gonxha. By the time she was twelve she was fascinated by missionary work and could remember every detail of what she had heard. One evening, at a church meeting, the parish priest pinned on the wall a map of the world with mission stations marked on it. To everybody's amazement the twelve-year-old Gonxha walked up to the map and began to explain to the audience the exact location of each mission and the work done there. She already knew that this was the kind of work she was called to do.

One day Mrs Bejaxhiu heard of a poor woman in Skopje who had cancer. Her own family refused to have anything to do with her and she had nowhere to go. Appalled, Gonxha's mother took her in and fed and cared for her until she recovered. Her daughter was always to remember that incident.

Acts like this fuelled her own resolve to become a missionary nun and to work for the poor. But she was happy at home and in no hurry to leave, so she didn't even mention what she had in mind until her eighteenth birthday. By that time she felt she dared no longer ignore what she was sure was God's plan for her life. When she broke the news her brother Lazar, who had just become a junior officer in the Yugoslav army, wrote her a horrified letter. Unperturbed, she wrote back: 'You think you are so important, as an official serving the king of two million subjects. Well, I shall be an official too, serving the King of the whole world.'

That was many years ago and she has never doubted since that she made the right choice. In any case, she

With her sister Aga (left)

9

Rathfarnham Abbey, Dublin

smiles, it wasn't her choice at all, it was God's.

So on 29 November 1928 the young Gonxha Bejaxhiu left her native land for ever and went first to Dublin, Ireland, where she was to join the Loreto Sisters at Rathfarnham Abbey. A few people there still remember her as a shy solitary girl struggling with the English language. But the most remarkable thing about her, they say, was that she seemed so unremarkable.

Dublin was just a stepping-stone. She stayed there only six weeks before setting off once again, this time for the country which was the focus for all her youthful dreams — India. She was to begin her life as a missionary in the hill station of Darjeeling.

2   Call within a Call

Darjeeling, famous for its tea, is in West Bengal, on the lower slopes of the Himalayan mountains. It is a health resort, and in the days when the British still ruled in India the Governor of Bengal and his staff and all who could afford to do so made their way to Darjeeling to escape the humid heat of summer. It was a fashionable, elegant place and holiday-makers there filled their days with dances, dinners, tea parties and long refreshing walks in the mountains.

But Darjeeling was also renowned as a centre for education, and it was to the Loreto convent that Gonxha Bejaxhiu came in 1929 to begin her missionary career, teaching the daughters of the well-to-do. Here, in 1931, she took her first vows as a religious Sister, changing her name to Teresa in admiration of the young French saint from Lisieux who was always known as 'the Little Flower'.

In many ways Darjeeling's beautiful mountain scenery reminded Sister Teresa of her native Yugoslavia, but such a comfort was not to be hers for long. Soon after taking her vows she was sent to the very different city of Calcutta, again to teach, but this time at a school run by the Loreto Sisters for Bengali girls — St Mary's High School, Entally. Sister Teresa was to remain there for twenty years, first as a teacher of history and geography and later as headmistress. By this time of course she had learned the Bengali language.

Teresa loved teaching and was immensely popular with the girls. And when six years later she took her

11

final vows as a nun, it seemed as though she had everything she had ever wanted. But something nagged away at her happiness, something she saw every time she looked out of her window at the convent. Beyond the well-kept green lawns, protected by the high walls, was one of the worst slums in the world.

Calcutta, India's largest city, is in the State of Bengal, which is steamy with damp heat, breathless and still. It is a city where very rich people live almost next door to beggars. Huge fortunes have been made out of its jute and other industries, but its slums are worse than anything that can be seen in the West. The homes of the poor are ugly mud huts or hovels made from petrol cans and covered with rough sacking or sheets of plastic. When it rains the mud stinks and the people are soaked to the skin. Many don't even have this kind of shelter: they live on the pavements, under bridges or inside huge concrete pipes; they camp out at bus or tram stops or on railway station platforms, surrounded by travellers, newsboys, water-sellers, rowdy children and the scream of trains. It is said that over a million people live — and die — on the streets of Calcutta, keeping themselves (barely) alive by begging, and sleeping in the open, covered with rags, newspapers or nothing at all. They scrabble in the city's garbage cans to find scraps of food or old newspaper to sell for a few coins, or for half-burnt lumps of coal which they clean up and sell for whatever they can get.

From her room at the convent, Sister — now called Mother — Teresa looked out onto the terrible swarming slum of Moti Jheel. The sight of whole families herded together in such squalor disturbed and depressed her. More and more she felt that the pleasant and enjoyable work she was doing was in distressing contrast to the needs of the slum-dwellers in Moti Jheel. She encouraged her older pupils in the Sodality youth group to go into the slums with food and to visit the hospitals. They then discussed what they had seen.

One day a beggar woman came to the convent door. Mother Teresa gave her some food, then put her into her own bed for the night. It saddened her that she could do so little to help her.

13

Then, on 10 September 1946, while she was on a train journey to Darjeeling, she suddenly knew that God was calling her to turn her life inside out. Suddenly she saw what she must do. It was breathtakingly simple. She must leave Loreto, leave the convent where she had been happy for so long, leave the school and her beloved pupils behind, and go and work in the slums. As she put it, 'I heard the call to give up everything and follow Him into the slums to serve amongst the poorest of the poor.' This was a call that could not be ignored. She did not feel that she had been offered a choice. It was a command. 'I knew it was God's will and I had to obey.' The 10th September is now known as Inspiration Day in the religious order she founded later on.

On her return from Darjeeling she went to see the Archbishop of Calcutta and told him that she wished to leave the Loreto Order. (A nun cannot just walk out of her convent. She must be given permission to do so.) Teresa told the Archbishop that God was calling her to serve the very poorest of Calcutta's slum-dwellers, the sick who were left to die on the city's pavements, the thousands of abandoned children who littered the streets. The Archbishop listened sympathetically but he would not agree to her request. She would not be strong enough for such a task, he declared. Besides, it was 1946 and India was on the eve of independence from Britain. A European woman dressed like an Indian, working in the slums, might be a target for considerable hostility.

Teresa was disappointed but not dashed. She could

As a young teacher at St Mary's High School, Calcutta. One of her pupils stands on her left

wait. If God really wanted her to go ahead, then she would certainly get permission in the end. Meanwhile she managed to get hold of some basic first-aid equipment — mainly aspirins and bandages — and went out onto the Calcutta streets with a handful of her Bengali pupils to start up a simple dispensary for the sick.

Twelve months later she went back to see the Archbishop, and this time he reluctantly agreed to let her take the matter further. She wrote to Pope Pius XII in Rome, telling him of her 'call within a call'. He replied by return, giving her leave of absence from Loreto for a trial period of a year.

Her way was now clear. With a mixture of joy and sadness, Teresa laid aside the black robes of a Loreto nun, and for 4 rupees (20p) bought a new 'habit', which was to become familiar all over the world — a cheap white cotton sari bordered with blue.

3 The Poorest of the Poor

It was 16 August 1948 when Mother Teresa left the sheltered life of Loreto behind and walked out into the unknown. She had been happy at Entally and the parting was painful. Her pupils wept to see her go. Why can't it be someone else, they asked. Why does it have to be her? When the time came for her to leave, the girls sang sad songs of farewell in Bengali. Mother Teresa cried with them, then went into the church to say a last prayer. From there, for the time being, she left Calcutta.

Her destination was Patna in the State of Bihar, over 600 kilometres away. Here she took a much-needed intensive nursing course with a group of medical missionaries. She had long ago realised that some sort of medical training would be necessary if she was to be of any use to the poor. Once on one of her forays into the Calcutta slums with her Bengali girls, a man had come to her with a gangrened thumb. Ignorant though she was, she could not send him away, so she got out a pair of scissors to cut the gangrene away. It is said that when she had finished, the man fainted one way and Mother Teresa the other.

Patna was to change all that. After four months there, Mother Teresa felt ready to return to Calcutta. She now wanted to found an Order of her own, one which would identify totally with 'the poorest of the poor', living exactly as they did. Her nuns, she told the medical missionaries, would eat only what the very poorest ate — rice and salt followed by salt and rice.

17

The medical nuns warned her that that would be stupid. How would they manage to help the poor if they too starved to death? Mother Teresa saw the point, and agreed that, when the time came, she would see to it that her nuns had enough food to keep them healthy.

She returned to Calcutta early in 1948 and found that the plight of the poor was even worse than before. India had gained its Independence in 1947, and with Independence had come the partition of the country into two nations, India and Pakistan, the former officially Hindu, the latter Muslim. Part of Bengal now lay in Pakistan, and the Hindus there, fearing massacre by the Muslims, were fleeing into India. Thousands of refugees poured into Calcutta's already over-burdened streets, adding to its desperate over-crowding and swelling the numbers of beggars and homeless.

With only 5 rupees in her purse, Mother Teresa set out upon her mission. At first she was given shelter by another Order, the Little Sisters of the Poor, but as soon as she could she rented a small room nearer to the slums. Each day she went out on foot into the slums of Moti Jheel and Til-Jala with medicines and a little food. And there in Moti Jheel, in the same slum which she had seen from the convent window, Mother Teresa now set up a school, outside, in a patch of ground among the wretched shacks. The slum children had never been to school, and indeed there was no school for them to go to, so they could neither read nor write. Mother Teresa had no tables, chairs, blackboard or chalk. But that did not deter her. Kneeling on the ground, she picked up a stick and began to trace the

Michael Gomes, who rented Mother Teresa a small room

Bengali alphabet in the dust. The children came off the streets and watched her, open-mouthed. That first day there were five of them but each day thereafter more and more came. They learned the alphabet and, starting with simple nursery rhymes, they learned to read and write. She also taught them simple hygiene, like how to wash with a bar of soap — something most of them had never seen.

When people realised what was going on, help began to pour in. Before long someone brought a table, someone else a chair, a third person a cupboard and so on. In March two of the girls from the Entally school, Subhasini Das and Magdalene Gomes, came to join her. And when on 7 October 1950 she received the long-awaited permission to found an Order of her own, these two were the first to offer themselves. Others followed, two or three at a time. 'It will be a hard life', Mother Teresa warned them. 'Do you think you can stand it?'

They were to be called the Missionaries of Charity, and they would wear the simple blue-bordered white sari of the poor, distinguished only by a small crucifix on the left shoulder. Their call was to see Christ in every single human being, the beggar lying in the gutter, the outcast made hideous by disease. In addition to the usual religious vows of poverty, chastity and obedience, Mother Teresa's nuns took an extra one — that they would give 'wholehearted and free service to the poorest of the poor', without ever accepting a reward. They could not, said Mother Teresa, understand the poor, if they were not willing to live among them and share their hardships.

So each nun was given two cheap white saris, one crucifix, a rope girdle, some rough underwear and a pair of sandals. These few things, together with a bucket to wash in and a thin mattress, would be their only possessions.

Subhasini Das became Sister Agnes (choosing Mother Teresa's own baptismal name) and Magdalene Gomes became Sister Gertrude. The life they led was very hard, and they had no money at all. Mother Teresa used to stand outside the church with a begging bowl, asking passers-by for their scraps, and the other Sisters begged for food from door to door. Perhaps it was quite natural in that city of beggars that they often found the

The street school was soon given a blackboard and chairs

door slammed in their faces. But as more people came to know what the Missionaries were doing, more came to offer help. Though Mother Teresa would not ask for money, voluntary contributions were made. The money, of course, was not kept for the Sisters' needs. Although Mother Teresa had not forgotten her promise to keep them healthy, their food was always of the most simple kind. The Sisters, she kept saying, 'have chosen poverty'.

21

4 Death on the streets

Mother Teresa was still quite unknown, and a beggar herself, begging for scraps of food and medicines for the poor from missionary societies, friends and total strangers. The clergy at her parish church gave her a corner for an outdoor dispensary and a well-wisher gave her five huge packages of medicines free. Everywhere she went she was surrounded by beggars and cripples pleading for help.

She began to look for a larger house to accommodate the growing number of Sisters — the number had grown to twenty-six. Trudging the streets, she became even more painfully aware of what the daily life of the poor was like. 'Today, while looking for a Home', she wrote in her diary, 'I walked until my legs and arms ached. I thought how the poor must ache in soul and body looking for food and a home.' On that occasion, and on many others, she longed for the comfort of the Loreto convent, but she put the longing firmly away from her.

Eventually, she had a stroke of luck. A Muslim gentleman who was emigrating to East Pakistan agreed to sell his house to her for less than the cost of the land on which it stood. At first she thought it too big, for it was on three storeys. But a friend persuaded her that one day the extra space might be useful. How right he was!

The Archbishop advanced the money and the rich Muslim's house at 54A Lower Circular Road, Calcutta, became the Mother House of the Missionaries of

Charity. That address is now famous everywhere in the world.

In this place the nuns prayed and meditated and learned how to care for the sick. 'Let there be kindness in you', Mother Teresa instructed them, 'kindness in your face, in your eyes, in your smile, in the warmth of your greeting. For children, for the poor, for all those who suffer and are alone, always have a happy smile. Give them not only your care but also your heart.'

One day, in search of medicines for her pavement clinic, Mother Teresa passed what seemed to be a child lying under a tree. Returning later, in the driving rain, she discovered the child was a shrunken and shrivelled old man, lying dead in a pool of his own vomit. 'They look after a dog or a cat better than their fellow-men', she cried, 'they would not allow that to happen to their pets.'

Death is a common sight on the streets of Calcutta. Every day, since her return to Calcutta, Mother Teresa had been coming upon corpses and reporting their discovery to the police. Then, one day in 1952, as she passed in front of a busy hospital in the city centre, she saw a woman lying on the pavement, not quite dead, her feet half-eaten by rats and ants. Without hesitation, Mother Teresa took the dying woman into her arms and carried her inside the hospital, where she demanded that the woman be admitted. At first they refused. The woman was too far gone, and anyway she was too poor to pay for treatment. The angry little nun persisted. She would stay there all day and all night too if necessary, until they agreed to take the woman in. At

Nirmal Hriday, the 'Place of the Pure Heart'

last her determination wore them down and the woman was grudgingly given a bed in which to die.

This small victory made Mother Teresa even more determined to help the destitute dying. From the hospital she marched straight to the town hall and asked for a place in which people could die with dignity and 'in sight of a loving face'. The town hall official listened in silence to her furious account of the woman and then took her to the temple of Kali, the Hindu goddess of death and destruction. Here there was a *darmashalah*, or pilgrims' house, where devout Hindus used to rest after worshipping the goddess. But it had long been used only by layabouts or drug addicts who had turned the place into a gambling den. 'You may have this place', said the official, and Mother Teresa promptly accepted. She was delighted to have a house near the Hindu temple, a place which was important to the Hindu people whom she served. She was aware that many poor Hindus already went to the temple of Kali to die.

Wasting no time, the Sisters moved in, and within twenty-four hours the first patients had been admitted. The work for which the Missionaries of Charity were to become famous had begun — the work of caring for the destitute dying of Calcutta. Some of the temple monks resented the intrusion of these Christian nuns, but one of them leapt to defend Mother Teresa: 'For thirty years I have been serving the goddess Kali in the temple', he said. 'But today I see before me the Goddess Mother in human form.'

The Home for the Destitute Dying was officially opened in August 1952. It was given the name Nirmal Hriday, the Place of the Pure Heart, though people simply called it Kalighat after the name of the temple. Every day the Sisters went out into the streets and brought back dying people, sometimes in a wheel-barrow. The first one to come was a woman found in a dustbin outside the hospital where Mother Teresa had staged her protest.

It was 'the poorest of the poor' the Sisters sought, those whom no-one wanted and who had no refuge at all. At Nirmal Hriday they were loved and cared for until they died. 'They lived like animals', explained Mother Teresa. 'At least here they die like human beings. We want to make them feel that they are wanted, we want them to know that there are people who really love them, who really want them, at least for the few hours that they have to live.' And one old man, on the edge of death, echoed her words when he said: 'I have lived like an animal, but I'll die like an angel.'

Help was not slow in coming. Doctors and nurses volunteered their services and more young women came along to join Mother Teresa in her work. The girls were Indian and Anglo-Indian, mostly middle-class, though a few came from the wealthy upper class. Some were still studying for their school exams and Mother Teresa diligently coached them. Most of them were her former pupils. Years before she had taken them one by one into the slums to show them the terrible conditions in which the poor had to live. Now they came to her, making what she described as 'a total surrender to God', giving up their possessions, their homes and families, their hopes of a career, and pledging themselves to the free service of those who had nothing. Some of them faced a great deal of opposition and even hostility from their families. It could not have been easy and without Mother Teresa's own great faith their courage might have failed them.

Their lives were hard. They rose at 4 in the morning and spent two hours in prayer before having breakfast. They cleaned the house and did the previous day's washing before leaving for the day's work at 8. As nobody stayed at home, they took turns at preparing a little food for the evening meal, finishing it off when they returned after the long day in the streets.

Some members of one Hindu sect resented the nuns'

presence in the temple and came to threaten Teresa's life. She looked at them quite calmly and said: 'Well, if you want to kill me, do it immediately, and then you'll send me to Heaven.' The answer surprised her attackers so much that they left. But others, too, feared that the nuns might want to convert the Hindu faithful to Christianity, an action forbidden by law. Local residents protested to the Calcutta Corporation and even to the

With Brother Andrew, leader of the Missionary Brothers

Sister Agnes caring for the sick

State Assembly. The nuns were pelted with sticks and stones as a warning. Finally a deputation of young men went to the Police Commissioner and asked him to drive out these unwelcome strangers. The Commissioner was sympathetic but insisted on seeing them for himself. Just as he arrived at Nirmal Hriday, Mother Teresa was tending a dying patient, applying potassium permanganate on dreadful sores which gave off a fearful stench. The Commissioner saw this — and more besides. He returned to the aggrieved young men. 'I have given my word that I will expel this woman and I will do so', he told them, 'but only on condition that you get your own mothers and sisters to do the work that she is doing.' The young men were angry with the

Commissioner, but he was adamant. 'At the back of this place', he said, 'is a black stone image of the goddess Kali, but there, inside that Home, is the living Kali.'

Even then the threats and stones continued, until the day when Mother Teresa found a young man in his middle twenties dying in a pool of filth outside the temple. Because he had cholera, which is infectious, nobody dared go near him, and no hospital would take him in. Mother Teresa went up to him, took him in her arms and carried him into Nirmal Hriday where she looked after him herself. Only later did she learn that the man was a temple priest, one of those who had bitterly opposed her presence there. The man himself was angry and resentful at first, but slowly his attitude softened and changed. 'He died very beautifully', Mother Teresa said afterwards.

And that finally put an end to the harassment. Word went round among the Hindus that the tiny nun with deep-set eyes and wrinkled face was not trying to convert them to Christianity. To her it did not matter whether a person was Hindu, Christian, Muslim or Buddhist. She cared for them all, regardless.

5 Dustbin Babies

One of the many stories which have sprung up around Mother Teresa tells of how she was once given ninety-five cartons of powdered milk. These were put out into the courtyard and almost immediately the rain came down in torrents and continued for five days. All this time the Sisters prayed anxiously that the milk would not be ruined. When the rain stopped and they went out to inspect the damage, it was found that though some of the cartons were torn or sodden, not one container of milk powder was wet.

On another day, one of the Sisters reported with dismay that there was no bread to give out. (They used to distribute loaves of bread each morning, most of them provided through the generosity of children in Britain). At that moment a lorry drew up, followed by a second. Both lorries were loaded with bread. For some reason, the government had shut down all the schools for one day and had decided to let Mother Teresa have the bread that the schoolchildren usually ate. 'There was so much bread', recalls Mother Teresa. 'All Calcutta ate bread for two days.' Stories like this give some idea of the respect and awe in which Mother Teresa and the Sisters are held. No-one is surprised by miracles — they happen all the time.

Each day, long lines of hungry people form outside a small door in a high wall. This is the entrance to Shishu Bavan, the working centre of the Missionaries of Charity. Inside, huge amounts of hot dhal (a puree of lentils) and rice are prepared. The hungry come to

eat, and sick people come too, knowing that they will find medicines and free treatment.

Shishu Bavan is only a few hundred metres from the spot where Mother Teresa found the first dying woman; it is also only a few hundred metres from the Mother House in Lower Circular Road. But there the resemblance ends. For the convent is bathed in peace and tranquillity and prayer, whereas Shishu Bavan is alive with noise and bustle and ceaseless activity.

Shishu Bavan is the nerve centre of Mother Teresa's work. It is not only where the hungry come to be fed and the sick to be treated. It is above all a home for abandoned or dying children. In this unimpressive four-storey building overlooking a concrete courtyard, there are children everywhere — on the stairs, on the landings, and outside. The Sisters claim that they have never turned a child away. 'We always have one more bed for one more child', they say. They take them all, the orphans, the crippled, the mentally handicapped, and those whose parents are simply too poor to keep them. Most of them are under-nourished or suffer from a dangerous chest infection called tuberculosis. Some have terrible sores or are covered with lice. Most have tragically thin arms and legs, and swollen stomachs. All of them are hungry for love.

These children would certainly die if Mother Teresa did not take them in, and many people criticise her for bothering to try and save them. There are too many people in India anyway, they say. Why not let some of them die? But Mother Teresa is fiercely on the side of life. 'I don't care what people say about the death rate', she protests. 'Even if they die an hour later, let them come. The babies must not die uncared for and unloved. Even a baby can feel. If we refuse them we are closing our doors and these babies will be killed.'

Many of the babies do die an hour later. Every morning, one of the nuns makes a heart-breaking journey to the hospitals, dustbins and garbage tips of Calcutta, and she never returns without at least one pitiful bundle. Sometimes there are three or four. Babies are abandoned on church or convent doorsteps, in clinics, or outside police posts. More often, they are just dumped in dustbins, drains or refuse heaps, like so much kitchen rubbish. Often they are brought to Shishu Bavan by social workers, doctors or the police.

In the Home the babies lie two or three to a cot, the very tiny ones with drip tubes in their noses because they are too weak to suck. The miracle is that so many of them survive to become healthy, happy children. In time, some of them are returned to their parents. Others are adopted either by Indian families or by families in other parts of the world. A few remain in Mother Teresa's care and she sees to it that they receive some kind of education or training for the future.

One little boy whose parents had died was brought by his grandmother to Shishu Bavan. In the years that followed, when anyone asked what he wanted to be when he grew up, he would reply, 'I am going to be Mother Teresa.' When he finished school, Mother sent him to a seminary and he became a priest.

A little girl called Sadhana was left at a railway station by her father. She stayed there for a night and a day, frightened and miserable, waiting for him to return. But he did not come back and she was taken to Shishu Bavan and brought up there. When she was old enough to get married, the Sisters found her a husband through a marriage broker (a Hindu custom) and Mother gave her a little house as a dowry. 'She is our child', she said.

On another occasion, a whole family of six became her children. The father had disappeared, the mother was dead and the eldest child, a girl of fourteen, was looking after the other children. Mother took them in and kept the family together.

Such love gives Shishu Bavan its special atmosphere. In spite of all the suffering that can be found there, the heartbreak of being abandoned, starving or sick, visitors to the Home return with one word usually on their lips. It is a *joyful* place, the exclaim in amazement. 'Joy' is one of Mother Teresa's favourite words. 'If you help the poor you must do so cheerfully', she has always insisted. 'You must take joy to their hearts.'

6 Driving out Fear with Love

In Calcutta they tell a story about Mother Teresa and a savage bull. They say that the bull was rampaging along a road where a group of lepers had congregated, and it had already gored an old man. It seemed as though nothing could prevent it attacking the other lepers. Then Mother Teresa came on the scene and stood right in the animal's path. She opened her arms, and the bull simply turned in its tracks and walked away quietly.

Lepers have always been cast out from society. We read in the Bible that they once had to beg outside the city gates, wearing a bell around their necks and shouting 'Unclean, unclean', to warn passers-by of their presence. Leprosy is a terrible, infectious disease and men have always feared it. It affects the skin, causing ugly sores, and it attacks the nervous system causing deformities and paralysis. The disease is usually only found where there is extreme poverty, malnutrition and homelessness.

All these conditions are met in Calcutta, and in this city alone there are 50,000 lepers. People who catch leprosy often hide the fact as long as they can for fear of losing their jobs, their families, their friends. And when the truth can no longer be hidden, the sufferer's worst fears are probably realised. His family deserts him and he has nowhere to go.

One day, in 1957, five lepers came to Mother Teresa for help. Their families had thrown them out, they had been dismissed from their jobs, they had no shelter and no food, and were reduced to searching for scraps in the city's garbage tips.

Mother Teresa set up a shelter for the lepers in a house at Gobra, on the outskirts of Calcutta, and one hundred and fifty of them came there. But the area was scheduled for redevelopment and the leper house had to be demolished. Mother persuaded the civil authorities to provide another site but, to her great disgust, the one they offered her did not even have water laid on. She was determined to fight for something better.

At that time leprosy was almost always treated in special hospitals, called leprosaria. But there were only a few of these and each one could take only two or three hundred people, whereas there were two or three million lepers in India. Also, lepers were reluctant to go into hospital, because they would then not be able to earn any money and their family might die of starvation.

Mother Teresa preferred the idea of small clinics. With the advent of a new drug, Dapsone, which enabled patients to be treated outside hospital, it became possible to set up small dispensaries where they could regularly collect their own medicine. The first of these was opened in September 1957 at Shishu Bavan, and within three months it had six hundred patients attending. Other similar centres followed.

To draw attention to the plight of the lepers, Mother Teresa started a Leprosy Fund and organised street collections. The collecting tins bore the words: Touch a Leper with your Compassion. It was an appeal for love and mercy as much as for money. When someone commented that he wouldn't touch a leper for a thousand pounds, Mother Teresa replied somewhat tartly that neither would she, 'but I would gladly do so for the love of God'.

While searching for another site for a leper clinic, she discovered a plot of land between two railway lines and arranged to go and see it with a friend. News of this plan leaked out and a hostile crowd of villagers was waiting for them. As they arrived, a village official shouted: 'Do you want a leper clinic here?' 'No', yelled the crowd angrily and, picking up stones and sticks, they began to hurl them at the two women, who were forced to retreat to their car. Mother Teresa was not in the least discouraged. 'Ah well', she sighed, 'I don't think God wants us to have a leper clinic in this place.

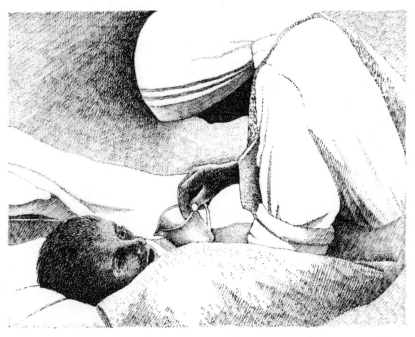

Caring for a dying man at Nirmal Hriday

37

We shall pray for two months and then we shall see what He does want.'

And guess what happened! During those two months Mother Teresa's prayers were answered in a highly dramatic way: a large electric light company gave her 10,000 rupees; a Hindu specialist in leprosy, Dr Sen, retired from his official hospital post and offered his services exclusively to Mother Teresa; and a group of well-wishers from the United States sent her an ambulance. These three things made possible a major advance in the care of leprosy sufferers by the setting-up of the first mobile clinic. This meant that from then on weekly treatment could be made available wherever there were large numbers of lepers. With Dr Sen in the ambulance went some of the Missionaries of Charity, trained now in leprosy care. They distributed medicines, free milk and rice, attended to the lepers' other ailments and above all tried to restore their self-esteem and self-confidence.

But this was not all. Out at Barrackpore, an industrial suburb of Calcutta, there were two hundred and fifty lepers with nowhere to go. The local Methodist minister wanted to open a clinic for them, but although he had a plot of land, he lacked the money to develop it. He approached the Anglican bishop, but he had no money either. The two men decided to go to Mother Teresa and offer her the land. The latter was delighted. At last, the Sisters would be able to have a permanent clinic. Today Barrackpore is known as Titigarh, and there are lepers living along both sides of the railway track, while the trains thunder by and rattle the bamboo walls of their shacks.

Since the Centre at Titigarh opened, thousands of lepers have been treated there as outdoor patients. Only those in an advanced state of the disease or who are highly infectious are admitted as indoor residents. At the Centre the lepers receive not only the drugs and medicines they need but also a vital training in self-help. They learn to weave their own bandages, to fashion shoes out of foam rubber and bits of old tyre, to make their own clothes and to do simple carpentry. The high-quality baskets they make are sent to the market, and they have a contract with the railways for making coconut-fibre matting for use on the trains.

When Pope Paul VI visited India in 1964, the

Two sisters visit a leper's cottage at Shanti Nagar, the 'Place of Peace'

American people gave him a luxurious white Lincoln Continental car to use throughout the visit. As he prepared to leave India, the Pope presented the car to Mother Teresa, 'to share', he said, 'in her universal mission of love.' No-one expected that a nun who had chosen to live the life of the very poorest would now drive around in a luxury limousine, and of course she did not. She gave the car to her helpers (called Co-Workers, as the great Indian leader, Mahatma Gandhi, also had called his helpers) and they raffled it, netting half a million rupees, five times its market price.

With this money she was able to realise a dream. The Government had given her a large site in a coal-mining area about 140 kilometres from Calcutta. Work had already started on this site, which she had christened Shanti Nagar, the place of peace. It was to be a settlement where lepers could live with something like normality. Money had already been sent in from all over India and from different parts of the world, and about thirty dwellings were already under construction. The raffling of the car meant that a vitally needed hospital could now be provided.

Shanti Nagar was planned as a rehabilitation centre where about four hundred leper families could live in an attractive setting and in relatively inexpensive but pleasant accommodation. It was to be a model leper village. Long before the lepers moved in, trees were planted, ponds stocked with fish, and every effort made to bring beauty into the lives of those whom the world thought ugly. The first to come were taught to make bricks and, armed with this knowledge, to build cottages for themselves and for later arrivals. The villagers became as nearly self-supporting as it was possible to make them. They planted their own rice crop, tended their own paddy fields, raised their own cattle and kept their own poultry. They wove baskets to sell and even started a printing press on which they could print leaflets and pamphlets. In true Indian fashion they adopted a system of village elders elected by the inhabitants themselves. The Sisters opened a shop on the site and before long the lepers were running it themselves. One man even set up in business as a tailor. The Sister in charge of Shanti Nagar brought him second-hand clothes which his deformed fingers were still clever enough to transform into new ones.

Today, Shanti Nagar is a bright and cheerful place with chintzy curtains up at the windows and bowls of flowers on the tables. The very sick lie in small, pleasant wards, while the majority live with their families in the little cottages they built themselves. A creche is provided for the small children of Shanti Nagar, and they are given special treatment to protect them from leprosy. It is a fact, though, that once the patients are on the way to recovery, very few of the children ever contract the disease.

The lepers are trained in new skills so that they are no longer condemned to beg for a living. Yet the greatest gift of all is the knowledge that they are not despised but loved.

7 These are our People

For ten years Mother Teresa worked only in Calcutta. All that time she was training and preparing her Sisters to work further afield. Throughout India the work of the Missionaries was becoming known and admired and it was not surprising that in 1960 the call came to send the Sisters to different parts of India. When Mother Teresa opened a children's Home in Delhi, the then Prime Minister, Mr Nehru, came to open it himself. When she offered to show him some of the work being done there, he said gently: 'No, Mother, it is not necessary. I know already. That is why I have come.'

In Bombay she offended some of the wealthy citizens by pointing out that their slums were even worse than those of Calcutta. Just after she arrived there, the newspapers carried the story of a woman who had died in a busy Bombay street and had lain unnoticed for hours. Mother Teresa wasted no time; before long Bombay had its own Home for the Dying Destitute.

She always refused to ask for money, saying 'God will provide'. He usually did. Once a Sister telephoned her from Agra saying that a children's Home costing 50,000 rupees was desperately needed. Mother Teresa said it was out of the question since there was no money. Let her tell the rest of the story: 'Then the telephone rang again. This time it was from a newspaper saying I'd been given the Magsaysay Award from the Philippines. I asked "How much is it?" The man replied: "About 50,000 rupees". So I called the Sister back to tell her that God must want a children's Home in Agra.'

But it wasn't just in India that the Missionaries had become a legend. Pope Paul had spoken of her 'universal mission of love' and it was indeed to become universal. 'There is no place in the world which is free from poverty and injustice', Mother Teresa had written.

By 1965 the Sisters and Brothers had been given permission to work outside India, wherever they might be invited. (There had been Missionary Brothers since 1963, with Brother Andrew as their Superior.) In that same year they went to Venezuela, to look after the old, to feed the hungry and, because of the drastic shortage of priests, to take Holy Communion to the sick. When, in 1972, a hurricane swept the coastline of Venezuela they took up roof-repairing as well!

Venezuela was only the beginning. Invitations flooded in from every corner of the world, sometimes from the local bishop but just as often from the Head of State. Since that time the Sisters, Brothers and Co-Workers have taken their labour of love to the Americas, the Middle East, Australia, Africa, Asia and Europe. Pope Paul VI invited them to Rome where they worked in a slum area among down-trodden Sicilian immigrants. They went to Sri Lanka, to Tanzania, to Jordan, and to the aborigines in Australia.

Teresa soon grew used to jet travel. In fact she rather enjoyed it. Nobody bothered her and she was able to say her prayers undisturbed. Once, when she was just beginning to travel and was short of money, she offered to work her passage as an air stewardess to pay for the flight. When the Prime Minister of India, Mrs Indira

Gandhi, heard of this, she arranged for Mother Teresa to be given an Air India free pass to anywhere in the world. (She already had a free pass on the Indian railways.) When travelling, it is her practice to collect the remains from the airline food trays to give to the poor.

Jet lag does not appear to trouble her. Nor is she in the least apprehensive about going where many others are afraid to go. Wherever there is flood, famine, earthquake or violent upheaval, the Missionaries of Charity are usually also there. In Gaza they have taken loving care to the Arabs living in Israeli-occupied territory, while once, in Jerusalem, a group of them narrowly escaped being shot as spies by Arabs who caught them as they passed from the Israeli to the Arab side. In strife-torn Yemen they were called 'carriers of God's love'.

To whatever land they go, the Sisters, Brothers and Co-Workers take the same message: that all human beings, no matter what their colour or religion, are God's children and must be shown His love. They tell the story in which Jesus said: I was hungry and you gave me food; I was thirsty and you gave me a drink; I was a stranger and you welcomed me; I was naked and you clothed me; I was sick and you visited me; I was in prison and you came to see me. The Missionaries of Charity look after the people with whom Jesus was identifying himself in this parable.

This is the reason why Mother Teresa turns her face towards the people whose needs are deepest. This is the reason why she isn't content just to open Homes but

44

must also provide clinics, dispensaries, mobile leprosy care, schools, creches, training centres, feeding programmes, commercial schools. The list is endless because the needs are endless. In the face of all human suffering Mother Teresa has tried to be a mirror for God's love towards the whole human race. Everywhere in the world she can say: 'The people who have nothing, who have nobody, who have forgotten what human joy is, who are rejected, unwanted, unloved, uncared for,

Displaying the Nobel Prize, presented by John Sanness, chairman of the Norwegian Nobel Committee

naked or homeless — these are our people.'

It is not surprising that she has been honoured by many countries with their highest awards. Of these, the best-known is one of the most prestigious prizes the world can offer, the Nobel Peace Prize, which Mother Teresa was awarded in 1979. 'It is a drop of deliverance in an ocean of suffering', she exclaimed when she was told of the award. Characteristically she added, 'Personally I am unworthy. I accept in the name of the poor, because I believe that by giving me the prize they have recognised the presence of the poor in the world.'

Nobody shared her belief that she was unworthy. The choice of Mother Teresa was a popular one and it was difficult to think of any prize-winner more deserving of the prize. The Indian Prime Minister, Mr Morarji Desai, expressed the feelings of many when he wrote of the Albanian nun who had served his country so devotedly, 'Many great people have trod this earth, but very few of these have been good people. Mother Teresa is good as well as great.'

She went to the Norwegian capital, Oslo, in December to receive the award — a tiny figure facing the bitter December weather in a cotton sari, carrying all her worldly goods in a shabby shopping bag, entering a world of pomp and glitter to which she did not belong, yet in which she was to be the most honoured of guests. After a service of thanksgiving held in the Lutheran Cathedral, a procession of about a thousand people with lighted candles walked through the streets of Oslo with Mother Teresa at their head. Their destination was a church hall, where a little girl handed her a

Giving the Nobel Prize address, Oslo, December 1979

cheque for $175, which had been donated by children all over Norway out of their own pocket money. Mother Teresa put her hands together and solemnly bowed in the Indian manner to express her gratitude. 'Yes, money is very necessary', she said to the children, 'but we must take care to increase its value by seasoning it with love.'

The Norwegians had risen to the occasion. A further $70,000 had been collected by the young people of Norway. And, to the disappointment of a few, Mother Teresa asked for the celebration banquet in her honour to be cancelled, the money ($6,000) to be spent on the poor and the lepers in India.

On 10 December 1980, in the presence of King Olaf of Norway, the award was made, and a cheque for the magnificent sum of $190,000 was handed over. As she rose to make her speech of acceptance, Mother Teresa asked all those present to recite with her the beautiful prayer used daily by all the Missionaries of Charity. And, in the name of peace, they all, whatever their religion, joined her in this prayer:

Lord, make me a channel of Thy peace,
that where there is hatred I may bring love;
that where there is wrong, I may bring the spirit of
    forgiveness;
that where there is discord, I may bring harmony;
that where there is error, I may bring truth;
that where there is doubt, I may bring faith;
that where there is despair, I may bring hope;
that where there are shadows, I may bring light;
that where there is sadness, I may bring joy.

Lord, grant that I may seek rather to comfort than to be comforted; to understand than to be understood; to love rather than to be loved; for it is by forgetting self that one finds; it is by forgiving that one is forgiven; it is by dying that one awakens to eternal life.

The Nobel Prize did not change Mother Teresa. Some months later she told a gathering in New York about a beggar in Calcutta who had given her a one-cent piece. 'He gave me more than the Nobel Prize', she assured them. 'He gave me all that he had. That is loving until it hurts.'

8 'You can't say No to a Saint'

Cyclones, famines, floods, riots — Mother Teresa had seen all of these and been quick to the rescue. But she had never been in a war. Not that is, until August 1982 when she went as Pope John Paul II's special envoy to Beirut in the Lebanon, where hundreds of thousands were starving, sick and homeless.

She had prepared the ground beforehand. At the end of July, during a visit to Britain, she had gone to visit her Sisters in Liverpool. Here an organisation called 'Survive', which sends medical vehicles to the Third World, presented her with a shiny new bus to be sent out to Cairo, in Egypt. Mother Teresa smiled and clapped her hands in delight when she saw the bus. But what she said took everyone's breath away by its sheer audacity. 'I must have one of these for Beirut', she told the administrator of 'Survive'. He gulped. 'I'll do my best', he stammered, wondering where on earth the money would come from and how many months it would take to collect. To Mother Teresa such worries were unimportant. To her it was crystal clear: if God wanted an ambulance for Beirut, then an ambulance there would be. 'Now', she said firmly, 'we need it now. There are children dying under the rubble in Beirut.'

'How can you say no to a saint?' asked the bemused 'Survive' official. So he launched another Appeal. Within three days, £3,000 had been raised. The money simply poured in as soon as people heard about Mother Teresa's request. 'It's absolutely unbelievable', said the organisers. 'We've never seen anything like it.' There was a constant stream of people into the office: one man had walked in with £100 in banknotes. The ambulance was well on its way. 'At this rate', said an official, 'she should have it in eight or nine weeks' time. It will be equipped with two stretchers and when not in use as an ambulance it can be used as a bus.'

With Pope John Paul II

On 10 August Mother Teresa was received by the Pope at his summer residence in the hills outside Rome. Pope John Paul had wanted to go to the Lebanon himself, but his advisers told him that this was out of the question. So when he heard that Mother Teresa intended to go there, 'to help the children, the handicapped and the war-wounded', he was very moved and decided that she must be his personal envoy. She had hoped to fly to any city from where she could reach Beirut, but now it was John Paul's turn to urge caution. 'You must go by boat', he insisted. 'It will be safer.' Together they knelt to pray that peace would come to the Lebanon and that a refuge might be found for the homeless Palestinians.

She flew from Rome to Cyprus and from there, obeying the Pope's injunction, boarded a boat going to Junieh, some 15 kilometres north of Beirut. The journey lasted seventeen hours. No doubt it was a tiring journey, but that did not stop her from getting to work as soon as she arrived in the ravaged city. Within twenty-four hours, she had rescued thirty-seven mentally retarded children from the chaos of a repeatedly-shelled hospital in West Beirut to the relative calm of a Christian school, which she had established two years earlier in the eastern part of the city. She was appalled by what she saw. 'I have seen famines and cyclones in India', she said sadly, 'but when I see all this I ask myself: "What do people feel when they do these things?" I do not understand at all how they can do it.'

o   o   o

London is a long way from Beirut and its tragedies are less obvious and dramatic. But its tragedies exist. When Mother Teresa first visited the city in 1970 she saw tramps sleeping rough, keeping out the winter cold with sheets of newspapers, and meths drinkers huddled beneath the railway arches. During this visit, too, she met a sixteen-year-old boy, weeping because his parents had thrown him out of their house. 'In England', reflected Mother Teresa, 'everyone looks prosperous, yet no-one looks happy.' She sat down and wrote a letter to her Co-Workers: 'For leprosy I have a cure', she wrote, 'for tuberculosis I have a cure. But for being unwanted and unloved there is no cure, unless there are willing hands to serve and a loving heart to love.' Those who asked her what they could do to help, she suggested, might look in their own neighbourhoods and on their own doorsteps for those who were in need, 'and bring them a heart to love and hands to serve, as my Sisters and Brothers would do if they were there'.

'Why don't you set up a convent in London?' Cardinal Heenan asked Mother Teresa. 'I'm already looking for somewhere suitable', she replied. In fact, she was looking in the district of Southall where there was a large Asian community. She went to view a house advertised for sale by a Jewish lady, but, at £11,000, it was too expensive. She could not go higher than £6,000, she told the estate agent, omitting to add that in fact she had no money at all. Next day the Jewish lady telephoned to say that she had spent many happy years in the house and wanted it to be 'filled with love' after she had left it; so she was willing to accept the £6,000 offered by Mother Teresa. Mother thanked her and then set off on a tour of the country, asking for prayers wherever she went. When she returned, she met Ann Blaikie, Chairman of her Co-Workers. 'Ann', she said, handing over her shopping bag, 'I think there's some money in there. Would you like to count it?' Mrs Blaikie did so, and found cheques and cash to the value of £5,995! Ann added the missing £5.

Going to receive her Honorary Doctorate from Cambridge University in 1977.
With her is Mrs Ann Blaikie

So the tiny nun in a blue and white sari came to London to offer the hand of friendship to its destitute men and women, to its down and outs, to its lost and lonely ones. She set up a Home for destitute women with twenty beds, where the Sisters provide meals throughout the day and try to provide a welcoming atmosphere. The women are able to stay as long as they like — days, weeks or months. There is a smaller day centre for men, and thirty or forty men come in off the streets each morning for a wash and shave, a cup of tea and a sandwich. In the evening they return for soup and more sandwiches. In Liverpool, the Sisters have a soup kitchen, where up to one hundred and fifty men come in each day, not just for a meal but for companionship. To show their gratitude, some of them once bought cans of paint and painted the chapel and the hallway of the convent.

The Missionaries of Charity now have three houses in London, one in Liverpool, one in Dublin and one in Glasgow. Each Sister has done her preliminary training in India, learning about every aspect of working among the poor. As Mother Teresa has always told them, 'You must really get to know the poor, because if you don't know them you can't love them, and if you don't love them, how can you serve them?' The Sisters' lives are as simple and spartan as ever they were in Calcutta. When they first arrived in London, Mother Teresa forbade them to eat the tinned vegetables which she imagined were a luxury. When it was explained to her that in Britain it was fresh vegetables which were luxurious, she withdrew the ban. The Sisters rise each morning at

Prince Philip congratulates Mother Teresa on receiving the Templeton Prize

5 o'clock to pray and meditate. By 8 o'clock they have breakfasted, done the washing and the housework. They then leave to do the work of the day. They go to the centres for the destitute or to the soup and sandwich run; they knock on the doors of the elderly and housebound, volunteering to do their shopping, clean their houses and attend to them if they are sick.

On 25 April 1973, at London's Guildhall, Prince Philip presented Mother Teresa with the Templeton Prize for Progress in Religion. She was the first person ever to receive the award and was selected from over two thousand nominees by an international jury. 'The sheer goodness which shines through Mother Teresa's life and work', said Prince Philip, 'can only inspire humility, wonder and admiration — and what more is there to be said when the deeds speak so loudly for themselves?' In reply Mother Teresa pointed to the continuing need:

'In England and other places, in Calcutta, in Melbourne, in New York, we find lonely people who are known only by the number of their room. Why are we not there? Do we really know that there are people like this, maybe next door to us? Maybe there is a blind man who would be happy if you would read the newspaper for him. Maybe there is a rich person who has no-one to visit him — he has plenty of other things, he is nearly drowning in them, but he needs your touch. . . . . . Let us not be satisfied with just giving money. Money is not enough, they need your hearts to love them. So spread love everywhere you go: first of all in your own home.'

9 Tell the children . . .

One afternoon, not very long ago, I went to call on Mother Teresa at the small convent which is her headquarters in London. Inside the simple terraced house in an ordinary London street, a number of people waited to see her. She made time for all of them, despite her busy schedule and the fact that she had only just arrived and would be on the move again the following day. When it was my turn, I told her that I wanted to write a book about her for children. 'Oh dear, there are so many books', she sighed. 'Too many books already.' Well, could she, I pressed her, make this one a bit different by speaking directly to all the children who might read it. Her face brightened. 'Yes', she smiled, 'tell them how important it is to share. Sharing is the most important thing in the world.' You might', she went on, 'tell them these stories, these true stories about other children'. And in her quiet voice which is the merest breath of a sound, scarcely even a whisper, she said:

Tell them about the little girl I picked up in a Calcutta street. She was about six years old and I could tell from her face that she was hungry and hadn't eaten for days. Then I gave her a crust of bread and she started to eat it, slowly, one crumb at a time. And I said, 'Eat the bread, go on, eat it'. And the child replied: 'I am afraid, because when the bread is finished I shall be hungry all over again.

That child could teach all children something. She is their sister.

In our schools in Calcutta we give free bread and milk to all the children, and I noticed one day that one little girl took her bread and hid it. I asked her why she was not eating the bread and she told me: 'My mother is very sick at home. We have no food in the house at all and I want to take this bread for her to eat.'

That is real love, real sharing, children could learn from that.

There was a little girl in America who had just made her First Holy Communion. She told her parents: 'I already have a white dress. Please send my Communion dress to Mother Teresa so that she can give it to a poor child.' The parents of that child wrote to me and said: 'It would not have occurred to us. Our little girl has taught us the joy of sharing what we have.'

A little boy in a wealthy family in Calcutta was having a birthday. His parents always gave him a lot of presents and a big party. This year he asked them to give all the money they would spend on him to Mother Teresa. And on the morning of his birthday they brought him down in the car and he handed me an envelope with the money in it.

That child taught his parents so much. That is love in action. Tell the children that. And tell them also that many children in Calcutta now do not invite their own friends to a birthday party. They come instead to our Children's Home and have the party there with our children as guests.

Mother Teresa has a special love for children

Tell them these things, she said, as my time ran out.
Persuade them to share, to 'love until it hurts.'

10 A Smile is the Beginning of Love

Mother Teresa of Calcutta is probably the best-known person in the world, yet she does not care a fig for fame. She shuns publicity for herself and hates to have her name in headlines. It was 'in the name of the poor' that she accepted the prestigious Nobel Prize for Peace, and on that occasion she said, as she has always said: 'It is not I who count. 'I am not important.' What is important to her is the plight of the rejected and unwanted, those whom the world has refused to love.

When she is given money, she buys bread for the hungry. If there is a lot of money she may open a new Home. But she will not worry beforehand about where the money is to come from. 'God will provide' is a phrase always on her lips. 'What is your budget?' a business man asked her. 'I have no budget' she replied. Then she corrected herself. 'Ah, you are my budget,' she told him. The man took the point, laughed and promptly wrote a cheque. Most rich people leave her presence poorer than when they arrived.

Once, in Rome, some Sisters had a sum of money stolen from them. 'Do not worry', she said, 'It's only money. The only thing we have to worry about losing is you and no-one's going to steal you — you're much too ugly. So get back to work now and forget about it.'

Mother Teresa started with courage, determination, and a great love — and that, together with a total faith in Divine Providence, was all that she needed. She began with 5 rupees in her purse and a twig for writing the alphabet in the Calcutta dust. Today her organisation is world-wide, but she is still the simple nun she always was. Her brother once told of an incident at Rome airport when the Italian ground staff were excitedly refusing to load the bundles of tinned food and assorted clothing which were bulging out of their wrappings of old newspaper and torn cardboard. Mother Teresa and her nuns ignored the fuss and knelt down calmly in the middle of the customs hall to pray. Then along came a different lot of officials who, with a shrug, agreed to take the bundles aboard. 'What were you doing?' asked the brother. 'Oh, we were just asking God to change the officials' mind', she answered.

Along with such simple faith goes a simple life-style. Her only possessions are two saris of coarse cloth and a bucket to wash them in. When she travels her luggage consists of a shabby shopping bag and a rosary. For shelter she has a cell which even in the humid heat of India does not boast a fan. (The electric fan in the convent in Calcutta is strictly for visitors only.) 'How can I tell the poor I love them if I do not live like them?' she asks simply.

She is, she says, 'a little pencil in God's hand'. It is the gospel of Jesus which she lives, and to do 'something beautiful for Jesus' is how she sees our human task. 'We see Christ in the slums and in the broken bodies of the forgotten people.' And the truly beautiful thing about Teresa and her Sisters is that they fulfil their task with so much joy. 'Let us always meet each other with a smile', she pleads, 'for a smile is the beginning of love.'

Not far away from her convent cell, the forgotten people of Calcutta have paid her their own special tribute. On a makeshift altar erected on a patch of dirt by the roadside and propped up against a tree, two statues of Jesus and his mother Mary are surrounded by candles and flowers. And on the tree there are coloured pictures cut out of magazines, of the street people's own personal heroine, Indian not by birth but by adoption, their very own saint — Teresa of Calcutta.

Prayer of Mother Teresa

Make us worthy, Lord, to serve our fellow-men throughout the world who live and die in poverty and hunger. Give them, through our hands, this day their daily bread; and by our understanding love, give peace and joy.

For information about the Co-Workers of Mother Teresa, write to:

> Co-Workers of Mother Teresa
> c/o Missionaries of Charity
> 177 Bravington Road
> London W9

or

> Co-Workers of Mother Teresa
> c/o Missionaries of Charity
> St Teresa's Church
> Donore Ave.
> Dublin 8